Trustworthiness

by Emily Lauren

RAINTREE
STECK-VAUGHN
RSVP PUBLISHERS

A Harcourt Company

Austin   New York
www.raintreesteckvaughn.com

Published by Raintree Steck-Vaughn Publishers, an imprint of Steck-Vaughn Company.

Library of Congress Cataloging-in-Publication Data is available upon request.

ISBN: 0-7398-5782-7

Printed and bound in China
1 2 3 4 5 6 7 8 9 10   05 04 03 02

A Creative Media Applications, Inc. Production

Photo Credits:
AP/Wide World Photographs: Cover
AP/Wide World Photographs: Pages 4, 6, 7, 10, 11, 12, 13, 15, 18, 21, 22, 23, 24, 25, 26, 27, 28, 29

Editor: Matt Levine
Indexer: Joan Verniero
Design and Production: Alan Barnett, Inc.
Photo Research: Yvette Reyes

Contents

"People may doubt what you say, but they will always believe what you do."

—Anonymous

Trustworthiness means that others can rely on you. It means that people believe what you say because they know that you are telling the truth. It means that your

Playing soccer together builds trust between these two girls.

friends know you are **loyal.** Trustworthy people are **honest.** If you are trustworthy, you are honest, **reliable,** and loyal.

People who are trustworthy have many friends. Other people have **respect** for them. People who are not trustworthy do not earn the respect of others.

A Trustworthy Friend

One day at soccer practice, Keisha shows her team the new CD player that she got for her birthday. When she arrives home after practice, the CD player is gone. Then the doorbell rings. Her teammate Amy is at the door.

Amy pulls the CD player from her backpack. She says, "I found this under the bench after practice. I had to go home first, but I brought it over as soon as I could."

Keisha thanks Amy again and again. She knows that Amy is a trustworthy person because she returned the CD player. Now she thinks that Amy would make a good friend.

Things to Think About

- What makes Amy trustworthy?
- What qualities of trustworthiness does Amy show?
- How might Amy have acted if she were not trustworthy?

If you are trustworthy, you deserve the trust of others. One of the best ways to show that you deserve trust is by being honest. If you are honest, people will know that you are trustworthy. A trustworthy person tries to be honest in everything that he or she does.

An honest person tells the truth. However, honesty is

An honest child, Conor Handolson, is rewarded with a check for $650. He turned in the money and no one claimed it. Honesty is the best policy even if you do not expect a reward.

Honest cabdriver Qurbe Munir Tirmizi appeared with David Letterman after he returned $32,859 to a 71-year-old woman. Tirmizi turned down the reward offered to him.

more than just telling the truth. Being honest also means playing fair, keeping your promises, and avoiding such things as stealing or hiding the truth.

Fifteen-year-old Stephanie DeNardi from Seminole, Florida, showed everyone in her town that she is both honest and trustworthy. Stephanie found a wallet on the street. It contained more than $400 in cash, plus credit cards and keys. Stephanie called the owner and returned the wallet and its contents. She said that it was "the right thing to do." Being trustworthy means that people can rely on you to do the right thing.

Trustworthy Means Truthful

When you tell the truth, you deserve to be trusted. Trust is something that can be earned. As people learn that they can trust you, they will rely on you even more. You become more trustworthy to them.

You cannot be a trustworthy person if you tell lies. Everyone knows that lying is wrong. Sometimes it might be hard to be completely honest. For example, you might tell a "white lie" to keep from hurting someone's feelings. However, telling the truth, even when it seems hard to do so, is a good example of showing trustworthiness.

Hiding the truth, or being **deceitful,** is also dishonest. A person who deceives others is just as dishonest as a person who lies. Another type of dishonesty is not telling the whole truth. This is called **omission.** A trustworthy person tells the whole truth without leaving out anything.

James comes into his house. His pants are dirty from riding his bike at the construction project nearby. He is not supposed to go into the work zone, but the dirt hills are perfect for bike stunts. His mother asks where he has been.

James says, "I was riding my bike with Khalil."

His mother looks at his pants. James knows that he has to make a choice. Should he tell the whole truth or make

You can earn someone's trust by telling the truth.
It is always best to tell the whole truth and not
leave out anything from your story.

up a story about the dirty pants? He knows that he will be in big trouble for going into the work zone. "There's more," he says slowly. "Khalil and I were bike-riding in the work zone. I'm sorry."

"It must have been hard for you to admit it," James's mother says. "You know it's dangerous. I have to ground you, but I'm glad you told the truth."

James feels relieved. At least his mom can trust him to tell the truth, even if he does not always make the right choices. By showing his mother that he can be trusted, James will gradually earn more **responsibility.**

Trustworthiness in sports begins with playing by the rules. The rules help everyone have a fair chance to succeed. All sports rely on the players, as well as the officials and coaches, to play within the rules.

Most children who play team sports try hard to follow the rules. If someone breaks a rule on purpose in order to gain an advantage, he or she is **cheating**. Bending or breaking the rules is a form of untrustworthiness in

The umpire has an especially tough job when making a close call. He is trusted to be fair to both teams.

Tom Kite is one of golf's champion players. He has a special love of the game.

sports. Cheating is always untrustworthy.

During a game, if a foul is committed by mistake, that does not mean that the player is untrustworthy. However, if a player commits the same foul over and over, then other players might question his or her trustworthiness.

Game officials try hard to be fair to both sides. An umpire or a referee might not get every call right. These mistakes do not make the officials dishonest or untrustworthy. The officials are doing their best, even when they make mistakes.

Tom Kite, a professional golfer, once was playing in an important tournament. He added a stroke to his score because he moved his ball a tiny bit by mistake. No one else but Kite saw the ball move. Kite knew that by the rules, he should be penalized one stroke. The object of golf is to take the fewest strokes to get the ball in the hole. Kite lost the match by one stroke. As a result, he lost thousands of dollars. However, he is known as one of the most trustworthy professional golfers in the game.

When you make a promise, you give your word that you will do something. Another person relies on you to keep your promise. That person counts on you to do what you say you will do. Reliability is an important part of trustworthiness.

The Los Angeles Lakers' Shaquille O'Neal slam dunks the ball like a real winner.

You make promises every day. Some promises seem small, such as coming home on time. Other promises are much larger, such as taking care of a younger brother or sister after school. Keeping any promise is one way to show trustworthiness.

As a professional basketball player, Shaquille O'Neal has won many awards. He was the National Basketball Association (NBA) Rookie of the Year in 1992. By 2001, he had won the league's Most Valuable Player (MVP) award and won two NBA titles with the Los Angeles Lakers. He was MVP

Shaquille O'Neal left Louisiana State University after three years to play pro basketball. He kept his promise to his family and himself to finish college. He is shown here at his graduation with his college coach, Dale Brown.

of the NBA Finals twice.

Shaq joined the NBA in 1992. To do so, he left Louisiana State University without receiving his college degree. He promised his parents and his college coach that he would one day return to get his Bachelor of Arts degree.

Shaq knew that he had to keep his promise. He spent eight summers studying and attending classes. Finally, on December 15, 2000, he received his college diploma.

Loyalty

Being trustworthy also means being loyal. Loyalty is a special trust that you give to certain people or groups. For example, most people are loyal to their families and friends. You probably also feel loyalty to your school, your sports teams, and your country. When you are loyal, you can be counted on as a trustworthy member of the group.

Loyalty is a two-way street. When you are loyal to your friends, you expect them to be loyal in return. You trust them, and they trust you. However, loyalty has limits. It is very difficult to be loyal to others if they are not loyal in return. You can feel different levels of loyalty. Loyalty to family can be very deep and last a lifetime. Loyalty to a sports team may last only for one season.

Ways to Show Loyalty to Your Country

- Fly the American flag.
- Stand when you sing the *Star-Spangled Banner.*
- Smile at a firefighter or police officer.
- Remind your parents to vote.

Players on the South Korean women's field hockey team depend on teamwork. They counted on each other as they played to a victory at the Centennial Olympic Games in 1996.

Loyalty to a country is called **patriotism**. Patriotism is a form of trust between you and your country. You rely on your country to provide freedom and a certain way of life. Your country relies on you to be a good citizen, vote, pay taxes, and support the government.

All loyalties are not the same. There are times when you cannot be loyal to everyone at once. For example, it is natural to put loyalty to your family above all other loyalties.

Trustworthiness at Home

When you are trustworthy, people know they can depend on you. Trusting your family members and being trusted by your family are especially important. You rely on your parents to provide a home that is safe and filled with the things you need to grow and mature. Your parents rely on you to follow basic rules and help with family matters.

Do You Trust Me?

On Saturdays Li's friends meet downtown at the library to do homework together. Li has asked her parents if she can join her friends. After a long talk, Li's parents agree that she can meet her friends this Saturday. Her parents are going to trust her, but Li has to agree to stay at the library.

On Saturday Li's father drops her off at the library. The other kids are waiting on the library steps. Her best friend, Josie, comes over and says, "We're going over to the new mall across town."

Li's parents are going shopping. She cannot reach them if she wants to change her plans. Her friends start walking away. Josie says, "Come on. They're leaving."

*These girls are at the library together. Their parents
trust them to go there to do their homework.*

Li takes a deep breath and says to Josie, "I told my parents
that I'd stay here. I can't go."

At first Josie looks disappointed. Then she says, "Me,
too. I promised that I'd stay here. I thought if you went to
the mall, I'd go, too."

Li and Josie wave to the other girls. "We have to do our
homework," they shout together. Then they both laugh.

Trustworthiness in school is important for learning. Basic trust among students, teachers, and parents is necessary for learning to take place. If any of these groups is untrustworthy, it affects the whole school.

Every day you show your trust for the people at your school. You use the playground, knowing that the

Students at Carrington Elementary School in Waterbury, Connecticut, show that they are trustworthy. They follow the hallway rules as they walk to the lunchroom.

Code of Conduct

This is a example of a code of conduct found in many schools.

- Be on time.
- Follow directions.
- Complete and turn in all assignments.
- Respect the rights and property of others.
- Be polite.
- Be honest and truthful.
- Dress appropriately for school.

equipment is safe. You eat the food in the cafeteria. You complete your work and know that it will be graded fairly. You may not realize it, but you expect your teachers and the school staff to be honest, reliable, and even loyal to you. You expect them to be trustworthy.

In return, teachers expect students to show loyalty to their school. They hope that students will be honest. They rely on students to do their best work. Many schools have adopted a code of conduct for students. These basic rules of behavior help students, parents, and teachers understand what is expected of them. By following your school's code of conduct, you show that you are a trustworthy student.

Who Is Trustworthy in the Community?

Nowhere is trustworthiness more important in the **community** than with emergency services. When you pull a fire alarm or call 911, you trust that someone will come right away. However, firefighters, police officers, and emergency medical workers trust that you will only call for help when you really need it.

Trust on the Ice

On January 3, 2002, Curtis Shattuck fell through the ice on the frozen Sugar River in Claremont, New Hampshire. The water temperature was only 36 degrees. Within a few minutes, the 11-year-old boy could die from loss of body heat.

The special cold-weather rescue unit rushed to the scene. Two firefighters put on cold-water rescue suits and crawled across the ice. They were in constant danger of falling into the freezing water and being swept away or dragged under the ice.

Finally one rescuer, Bryan Burr, reached the boy and pulled him onto the ice. Slowly they made their way back

Resources

Bauer, Margaret Dane. *A Question of Trust.* New York: Scholastic, Inc., 1994.

A boy and his younger brother cope with their mother's leaving by caring for a stray cat and her kittens.

Paterson, Katherine. *The Great Gilly Hopkins.* New York: HarperTrophy, 1987.

After many bad experiences, 11-year-old Gilly finally learns to trust through the support of a special foster mother.

Steig, William. *The Real Thief.* New York: Farrar, Straus and Giroux, 1973.

A thief must deal with his guilty conscience when Gawain the Goose is falsely accused and punished for stealing.

www.annefrank.com

Click annefrank: her life & times. Then click timeline, scrapbook, or diary excerpts to learn more about Anne Frank's life.

Index